D1189170

Schools of Citizenship

Schools of Citizenship: Charity and Civic Virtue

Frank Prochaska

Civitas: Institute for the Study of Civil Society
London

323.60942
P

First published April 2002

© Frank Prochaska and
The Institute for the Study of Civil Society 2002
The Mezzanine, Elizabeth House
39 York Road, London SE1 7NQ

Cover illustration, 'Freedom of Speech' by
Norman Rockwell, printed by permission
of the Norman Rockwell Family Agency.
© 1943 the Norman Rockwell Family Agency
Collection of the Norman Rockwell Museum at
Stockbridge, Norman Rockwell Art Collection Trust

email: books@civitas.org.uk

All rights reserved

ISBN 1-903 386-19 5

Norman Rockwell's 'Freedom of Speech' was one of a
series called The Four Freedoms, the other three being
'Freedom from Want', 'Freedom from Fear' and 'Freedom of Worship'. They were created in 1943, inspired
by a speech given by Franklin D. Roosevelt, and
toured America raising money for War Bonds. $133
million worth of Bonds were sold, and over four
million copies of the images were distributed world-
wide.

Typeset by Civitas
in New Century Schoolbook

Printed in Great Britain by
The Cromwell Press
Trowbridge, Wiltshire

*Among democratic nations it is only by associa-
tion that the resistance of the people to the government can ever display itself; hence the latter
always looks with ill favour on those associations
which are not in its own power; and it is well
worthy of remark that among democratic nations
the people themselves often entertain against these
very associations a secret feeling of fear and
jealousy, which prevents the citizens from defending the institutions of which they stand so much
in need.*

*Alexis de Tocqueville
Democracy in America (1840)*

CARDIFF UNIVERSITY
16 MAY 2002
PRIFYSGOL CAERDYDD

This publication has been made possible
by a generous research grant from
the Earhart Foundation

The author and publisher would like to thank
Leonard P. Liggio,
President of the History and Economics
Research Foundation, for his support and assistance

Contents

Author

Frank Prochaska is the author of several books on
the history of British philanthropy, including *Women
and Philanthropy in Nineteenth-Century England*
(1980), *The Voluntary Impulse: Philanthropy in
Modern Britain* (1988), and *Royal Bounty: The Making
of a Welfare Monarchy* (1995). His most recent book is
The Republic of Britain, 1760-2000 (2000). He is a
Lecturer and Senior Research Scholar in the Depart-
ment of History, Yale University, and a Senior Research Fellow at the Institute of Historical Research,
London University.

Foreword

In the days when people thought in a more allegorical way, it was not unusual for artists to depict ideas in triumphant form. The seven sacraments, the divine right of kings, the blessings of empire, commerce, education, truth and valour have all had their respective triumphs in paint and plaster, marble and masquerade.

We are less inclined to talk in terms of the triumph of this or that nowadays, although, as the economist Maynard Keynes famously observed, ideas are no less potent. 'Indeed, the world is ruled by little else.'[1] The decades following the Second World War saw the triumph of planning, as people looked to the state to provide them with everything from health care and education to transport and telecommunications. When the inadequacies of the state as omni-provider became apparent, the 1980s saw the triumph of the market. The discipline of the market was seen as the remedy for the inefficiency and remoteness of the state. This modern Manicheanism in which the whole world was divided between good (the market) and evil (the state) failed to satisfy, as it conflicted with most people's experience of life. There are some things—in fact most of the best things—on which you cannot put a pricetag.

And so the 1990s saw the emergence of several attempts to find some space between the state and the market: a third way, or third sector, or some species of communitarianism. Out of this suburb of half-way houses came a renewed interest in the concept of civil society as a conglomeration of institutions which mediate between the individual and the state. The family, the churches, professional associations, charities and self-help initiatives all found themselves part of this new idea—which in reality was not so new at all. Civil society was promoted as the answer to the social ills which divide us: its component parts would make us self-supporting, altruistic and energetic citizens. Not surprisingly, the idea was pounced upon by members of all political parties, who tried to co-opt it into their manifestos. In the process, it has undergone some strange transformations, as noble concepts tend to do when politicians get hold of them.

We therefore decided to ask Frank Prochaska to write this essay for us on the history and significance of the idea of civil society. Dr Prochaska is, in every sense, the ideal author for such a study. He is the historian of English philanthropy, whose books have transformed the way in which we look at the subject. In his first book, *Women and Philanthropy in Nineteenth-Century England* (1980), he drew on extensive research through historical archives to show that philanthropic work offered women opportunities for leadership, entrepreneurship, financial management, hands-on delivery of services and a place in policy debates which would not have been open to them through any other channels. *Royal Bounty* (1995), his history of the involvement of the Royal Family with charity, threw new light on the significance of the voluntary sector for a constitutional monarchy. His most recent book, *The Republic of Britain* (2000), demonstrated that republicanism is not necessarily the enemy of monarchy but of tyranny. Many advocates of republicanism, at least in the British tradition, have seen voluntary action as a vital means of developing those civic virtues on which a republic depends, and if that meant having a Royal patron to drum up support for a charity, then so be it.

Dr Prochaska's experience in these related fields has enabled him to untangle the sometimes confusing and rival interpretations of civil society, which he describes as 'among the most fertile, if amorphous, concepts in history' (p. 4). He is able to show that the notion of civil society as a clearly defined space between citizens and the government is of relatively recent origin, given an early expression in Thomas Paine's *Common Sense* (1776). Paine drew an important distinction between voluntary associations and government. The former promote our happiness, the latter restrains our wickedness. Voluntary action has been seen as a mainstay of a free and open society ever since, providing 'a moral training and experience in the democratic grass roots' (p. 6). It is an important component of a free-market economy, 'the human face of capitalism' (p. 8). However, as the state took over more and more of the functions of voluntary associations, the institutions of civil society were weakened. They lost many of their functions, and much of their influence on the formation of character. At the same time, as Dr Prochaska astutely points out, the centralising tendencies of the collectivist state actually disempowered people who no longer had the opportunity to do things for themselves at a local level and on their own initiative. 'The more ... politicians talked about the people and the national community, the weaker people and communities became' (p. 37).

And now, it's all change again! Suddenly politicians are enthusiastic about the small platoons, and want to enlist their support. Chancellor Gordon Brown, who, in 1988, decried charity as 'a sad and seedy competition for public pity', now wants to re-invigorate charitable service (p. 42). He admits that the mother in a playgroup may know better than the man in Whitehall. However, charities, and indeed all of the institutions of civil society, should be wary of the ambiguous embrace of the state. As Tocqueville reminds us, in the brilliant passage which forms the epigraph to this book, governments don't really like organisations which are outside their control. That is why they try to deal with the inconvenience, in the old days by prosecution and prescription, in modern times by subsidy and regulation. There is much talk today in the voluntary sector of a 'compact' with the state. This could turn out to be the sort of compact which the oysters had with the Walrus and the Carpenter: it ends up with one party getting eaten by the other.

By publishing *Schools of Citizenship*, we hope to join with Alexis de Tocqueville in encouraging citizens to defend 'the institutions of which they stand so much in need'. This is the sort of short book which can only be written by the author of several long ones. It draws on a lifetime of reading, writing, talking and thinking. It distils the history and literature of nations to make profound points in an elegant and epigrammatic prose style which has almost vanished from the groves of academe. Civil society is due for a triumph of its own, with Frank Prochaska amongst its laureates.

Robert Whelan

1

A Great Army of Busybodies

The poor will always have us with them. And charitable action has been hallowed since antiquity. But in Britain at different times, charity has been taken by champions of the working class to be subversive of their independence, and by promoters of the all-embracing state to subvert the progressive plans for democratically elected governments. Subversion is in the eye of the beholder. Clearly, charity can lift or depress the spirits. At its best, it is an expression of altruism and personal service, wholesome and redemptive, not least to the giver. At its worst, it can be little more than a kindness that kills, adversarial and punitive, not least to those on the receiving end. In the creative chaos that has always marked charitable campaigning, one person's philanthropist can be another person's killjoy. But whatever one thinks of the charitable, no one can deny their historic social engagement. It is worth recalling A.J.P. Taylor's observation that voluntarists, 'a great army of busybodies, ... were the active people of England and provided the ground swell of her history'.[1]

In mid-Victorian Britain, a sense of philanthropic duty to the community prevailed over any assertion that the deprived had a right to national assistance. A hundred years later, government had taken over much that previously had fallen to the charitable services. By the 1960s, charity was widely seen as little more than an amenity, a rung on the ladder leading to the welfare state. The ideological battle which took place between voluntarists and collectivists in the twentieth century appeared to have been won by the latter. The long-running policy debate largely turned on the role of government in shaping a social democracy. On one side stood those who advocated traditions of personal service and the participatory, 'subscriber' democracy inherent in local voluntary institutions; on the other side were those who advocated collective provision and central government control. As both parties were given to self righteousness, there was little love lost between them.

> *'The ideological battle which took place between voluntarists and collectivists in the twentieth century appeared to have been won by the latter'*

Ultimately, one's view of charity is political, for it raises the thorny issue of how a society should be administered. Much in political life turns on usage, and the political classes, attuned to shifts in public opinion, are continually redefining words with a view to reaction or reform. What, for example, do the words socialism or conservatism, left or right, mean today? Charity has not been immune to changes in usage. Most Victorians thought it to be the most wholesome way of promoting individual reformation and social harmony. Even if writers such as Dickens drew attention to the misguided activities of 'morally tidy' campaigners, charity was an essential sphere of social relations. Throughout the nineteenth century, it was widely seen as an expression of local democracy and civic pride, of hope and aspiration.

To twentieth-century collectivists, on the other hand, charity was a distasteful conceit, redolent of hierarchical values and unfashionable pieties. Charity remained alive among individuals and institutions, but most policy makers and social theorists took the view that it was socially divisive and irrelevant to the needs of the poor. For decades, a school of historians demonised philanthropy as a form of 'bourgeois hegemony', a thinly disguised form of self-interest, which was at odds with working-class culture and socialist transformation.[2] To those who interpret society in terms of class conflict, the very idea of *noblesse oblige* is an insult. A proper social democracy, argued Barbara Castle, a former Labour Minister of Health, should show 'a toughness about the battle for equality rather than do-goodery'.[3] The use of 'do-gooder' as a term of abuse encapsulated a transformation of values.

> *'But with collectivism in retreat, fewer people now look to the state for the cure of all social ills or see state planning as the road to freedom'*

In the heyday of state-directed services in Britain, people often dismissed charity without thinking of the political benefits of voluntary activity. In so far as welfare was perceived as synonymous with government provision, it was assumed that the poor had little hope of improving their condition without reference to the state. But with collectivism in retreat, fewer people now look to the state for the cure of all social ills or see state planning as the road to freedom. Many are alienated by faceless bureaucracy and what they see as an erosion of participatory democracy. Consequently, there has been a revival of interest in charitable service, a tradition in which citizens are seen as having duties as well as rights. In the years ahead, it seems unlikely that perceptions of philanthropy will be reduced again to middle-class deceit or a stage on the way to the welfare state.

The revival in status of British charity cannot be explained simply by reference to disenchantment with state bureaucracy, cuts in statutory services, or the fiscal incentives to the voluntary sector supplied by successive governments. It also has to do with the language of politics, which is reshaping the context in which charity is understood. Importantly, charity has been elided with notions of civil society or community service in the last decade. Consequently people feel more comfortable with it. Since the collapse of the Soviet Empire in 1989, an interest in civil society has grown enormously in Britain, as elsewhere. Western societies have been reminded of the democratic and social benefits of voluntary institutions. Once taken for granted, civil society is now so topical that it has become the common ground for both civic socialists and civic conservatives.

> *'civil society is now so topical that it has become the common ground for both civic socialists and civic conservatives'*

Civil society is among the most fertile, if amorphous, concepts in history, for it deals with the possibilities of sociability and the boundaries of politics. As a writer in the *Economist* reports: 'it is universally talked about in tones that suggest it is a Great Good', in part because it is 'often mentioned in the same breath as democracy'.[4] Nowadays it usually refers to a separate sphere, a half-way

> *'As a buffer between the government and the citizenry, civil society promotes a moral environment in which individual rights and civic virtues, essential to social well-being, may be expressed'*

house of free associations between the state and society, which mitigate the atomising effects of both bureaucratic government and the market. As a buffer between the government and the citizenry, civil society promotes a moral environment in which individual rights and civic virtues, essential to social well-being, may be expressed.[5] As one theorist puts it, 'it has the potential of making all our societal relationships rather less than totally obvious... It can offer new routes of freedom by showing that the world does not have to be like it is'.[6]

Families and neighbourhoods are often seen as crucial to civil society, for they provide the most immediate protection in a hazardous and uncertain world. Charities, community organisations, trade unions, pressure groups, think tanks and other non-governmental organisations are among civil society's other institutional forms. All of them operate within a pluralist political culture and are an expression of free association, individual rights and formal legality.[7] But as Brian Harrison points out, it cannot be said that all voluntary organisations, particularly those dedicated to single issues, are 'in every respect pluralist in their ideals, instincts or impact'.[8] Interest groups are not always tolerant of open discussion. Many are self appointed and unaccountable. At the extremity, they may even pose a threat to the democratic process through the promotion of violence or direct action. There is a type of voluntarism, it should be said, that undermines the very civil society that sustains it, a point that events in America on 11 September have made more obvious.

Charities are by definition less self-interested than other types of voluntary organisation. They are 'untidy and imperfect', as Ralf Dahrendorf observes, but they nonetheless contribute to a more 'prosperous, civil and liberal world'.[9] Many of them have an implied politics, and some lobby government within the framework of traditional legislative procedures. But under existing law a political purpose is incompatible with charitable status, though the question as to whether ancillary political activity is permissible is less clear. Of the 180,000 institutions registered with the Charity Commissioners in Britain, few resort to direct action. Their operations are part of the democratic process, 'a badge of citizenship' as the Commission on the Voluntary sector put it in 1996.[10] Not all of them can be called 'subscriber democracies' (many have been run by autocrats), but at their best they provide a moral training and experience in the democratic grass roots.

2

Charity and Republican Virtue

Over the centuries republicans and classical liberals have insisted that a vibrant civil society, however defined, requires a high degree of civic virtue to sustain it. Civic virtue is, of course, the foundation of republican thought, which enshrines free institutions outside the state. Charitable institutions may be seen as an embodiment of what has been called 'civic republicanism'. The phrase is coming into prominence in Europe and America, where it is increasingly believed that charities and other voluntary institutions should play a more prominent role in national life. Drawing on eighteenth and nineteenth-century sources, today's political scientists see the taproots of republicanism in self-government and civic spirit, a willingness to join with others in the promotion of the commonwealth, or in modern usage, liberal social democracy. A specific quality necessary to promote the common good is a desire to act charitably, for the virtue of charity contributes not only to individual happiness but to social integration.

'Current definitions of civil society draw on ancient ideas of republican citizenship infused with Christian notions of social justice and benevolence'

Current definitions of civil society draw on ancient ideas of republican citizenship infused with Christian

notions of social justice and benevolence. Civic republicanism, despite its secular associations, has often
been driven by religion.[1] Radical literature is dotted
with references to 'Christian republicans', who es-
poused Christ's doctrine of 'love' and 'charity'.[2] Charitable activity has been all the more intense in Britain
because of religious allegiances, which have encouraged a flowering of institutions
competing for converts and custom.

> **'The free enterprise
> of philanthropy is
> ... the human face
> of capitalism'**

There is a strong linkage between
charity and free enterprise, as
there is between civil society and
free enterprise generally. The free
enterprise of philanthropy is, in a
sense, the human face of capitalism, addressing the
social and individual ills which capitalism often
creates. In the communion of Christianity and commerce, civic virtue echoes the Calvinist's suspicion of
wealth, which encourages giving some of it away.
Much charity may be seen as civic republicanism
turning its mind to social conditions under religious
pressure.

Res publica, of course, simply means the 'public
thing', a malleable concept which succeeding genera-
tions have linked to progress or the public good.
Though a protean idea, it has enduring associations
not only with civil society but with the expansion of
democratic rights. In contemporary America, where
the concept of republican virtue has re-emerged, it is
associated with participation in such causes as multi-
culturalism, women's rights and environmentalism.[3]
In contemporary Britain, the word 'republic' has been
hijacked by anti-monarchists; but the core of republican thought still resides in individual freedom and
public spirit, which sustains a vibrant civil society.

Wherever they are found, democratic republics, whether presided over by a monarch or a president, require a high degree of engagement by the citizenry. Historically, most republicans have been less interested in government forms than the rule of law and a vision of virtuous citizens creating a higher, risen life.

With its foundations in communal bonds and public spirit, civil society, like republicanism, is protean. Our present vision of civil society, in which voluntary institutions mediate between the individual and the state, has relatively recent ideological origins. Classical, early Christian, and neo-Roman authors saw little value in the creation of a separate sphere of voluntary institutions as a buffer against government.[4] When classical republicans discussed civil

> *'most republicans have been less interested in government forms than the rule of law and a vision of virtuous citizens creating a higher, risen life'*

liberty, they thought of it in high political terms. And when they described public spirit they thought of it in terms of political or military service. They were, as Quentin Skinner puts it, 'innocent of the modern notion of civil society as a moral space between rulers and ruled'.[5] But an important ideological shift was taking place in the eighteenth century over the application of republican virtue. In an era of urban growth and democratic stirrings, the idea of civic virtue had moved on among the politically articulate. The city itself had always been an element of civil society.[6] But to the citizens of late eighteenth-century London or Philadelphia, civic republicanism did not mean the same thing as it did to citizens of ancient Rome or renaissance Florence.

In his great polemic *Common Sense* (1776), the republican Thomas Paine drew the important distinction between government and civil society. Indeed, his most recent biographer argues that the pamphlet was 'the first political essay in modern times to make and defend the distinction ... between civil society and the state'.[7] To Paine, the state was an artificial contrivance, 'the badge of lost innocence' as he famously put it. Voluntary institutions, on the other hand, opened up visions of reform based on man's natural sociability. 'Society', he wrote, 'is produced by our wants, and government by our wickedness, the former promotes our happiness positively by uniting our affections, the latter negatively by restraining our vices. The one encourages intercourse, the other creates distinctions. The first is a patron, the last a punisher'.[8] Paine was part of a movement of ideas that was giving shape to a vision of citizenship that recognised participation in voluntary, non-governmental institutions as a test of republican virtue. This was in keeping with commercial expansion and the massive flowering of civic and charitable institutions taking place at the time.

> *'Society is produced by our wants, and government by our wickedness'*

Paine may be seen as a bridge between the moral community of civic republicans and the rights-based culture of liberal individualism. His ideal republic, a land of liberty free from arbitrary rule, could only flourish through civic virtue embodied in free associations outside government control. Like many radicals, Paine spoke more about rights than duties, and he expressed his own civic spirit through political association rather than benevolence. But, as he knew, political association invigorates civic life generally.

The active citizenship valued by all republicans, whatever their stripe, was communitarian in outlook, emphasising the bonds that linked autonomous individuals. It found expression in the array of voluntary societies, not least among them charities, which appeared in ever increasing numbers in the nineteenth century. In an urban, commercial society, a viable republic depended on active citizens placing the good of the community before their own self-interest. Happiness itself was the product of social engagement or participatory virtue.

For centuries, voluntary bodies have been at the cutting edge of social and political action, whether they were charities for the poor, societies for mutual aid, religious associations, or radical debating clubs. They spread information, stimulated debate, and provided essential services. Moreover, they were seen as a check against

> 'the more we rely on ourselves, the smaller our need for the state'

bloated, uneconomical government, a cause dear to reformers of various political persuasions. The promotion of decentralised government, it should be emphasised, was a principal object of British republicans, or Commonwealthmen, after 1688. It remains so today among Paineite republicans, who often look to the regeneration of civil society for social and political transformation. The current emphasis on devolution and responsible citizenship in Britain carries forward the ideals of a democratic republic. As the republican writer Jonathan Freedland argued in *Bring Home the Revolution; The Case for a British Republic*: 'the more we rely on ourselves, the smaller our need for the state; the smaller the state, the more we will learn to work together'.[9]

Democracy comes in different forms, and in the past it did not necessarily mean majority rule or popular sovereignty. Paine advocated representative democracy for larger political communities; but, like Samuel Taylor Coleridge and Alexis de Tocqueville, he believed local institutions outside government control embodied self government.

Democracy is immanent in institutions. Many voluntary societies, of course, were not inspired by a faith in democracy, and some of them had little enthusiasm for the participation of the membership for reasons of confidentiality.[10]Nevertheless, most charities encouraged habits of association and may be seen as an expression of democracy in the sphere of social and moral reform. Institutional self government, it was argued, not only provided a check on the mechanisms of the central state—and the tyranny of the majority—but guaranteed peaceful competition and solidarity based on shared interests. As Tocqueville, the great theorist of associational democracy, argued: 'The greater the multiplicity of small affairs, the more do men, even without knowing it, acquire facility in prosecuting great undertakings in common.'[11]

As a focus for communal values, charities attract, as they have always done, individuals from differing backgrounds to co-operative ventures. While bringing together people with little in common beyond an interest in a cause can create friction, voluntary bodies often help to break down personal barriers and reduce social fragmentation. Those open to the general public have sufficient flexibility to permit people to join or to resign at will. With public meetings and elected committees, they are run with a minimum of interference or contractual obligation, though this is being subverted today by increased government funding. In the past at least, they could achieve their *ad hoc* purposes without being stifled by ritualised conventions or immobilised by politics. As proponents of civil society argue today, the fluid, instrumental traditions of voluntary association insulate nations from collectivist utopias and make a rigid, monopolistic political system less likely to develop.[12]

A democratic process takes hold in the seemingly inefficient muddle of charitable activity. Take the practice, once common among British charities, of electing beneficiaries by the vote of subscribers. The Victorians sometimes criticised these 'voting charities' as anachronistic, but such institutions sharpened the significance of participation and had the merit of making personal bonds between the giver and the receiver of assistance. Typically, a committee drew up a list of candidates eligible for relief, and all the subscribers then voted, each casting his or her vote proportional to the amount of his or her subscription. The practice may have been, as Florence Nightingale complained, 'the best method for electing the least eligible', but it embodied a democratic process, however corrupted by 'electioneering'. Indeed, for many benefactors, particularly women, they were the only votes available to cast. As the managers of the voting charities insisted, the freedom to contribute directly to charitable outcomes also brought in subscribers.[13]

Whether conservative or radical, driven by paternalism or individualism, charitable campaigners have commonly assumed that free associations give a voice to subscribers and civic leaders and a hand up to the needy, while acting as a counterweight to government. Among the most consistent arguments in favour of charitable activity is that it promotes self-help and local independence and offers an alternative to uniform assistance. (These points were often made by defenders of the voluntary hospitals before they were nationalised in 1948.)[14] Seen in this light, philanthropic bodies, like other voluntary associations, are bastions of democratic pluralism, an expression of both the rights and duties of republican citizenship. Associational philanthropy carries forward the ancient obligation of civic duty within a commercial society, with its accent on individual autonomy. As 'schools of citizenship', to use Tocqueville's phrase, charities, like debating clubs or societies for mutual aid, are part of the process of encouraging and diffusing local democracy. As nineteenth-century republicans believed, local autonomy serves not only as an antidote to standardising bureaucracy, but helps to heal social divisions, for it encourages class co-operation at the local level.

> '*philanthropic bodies ... are bastions of democratic pluralism, an expression of both the rights and duties of republican citizenship*'

Take an example of an institutional expression of civic republicanism in the nineteenth century, which brought together a motley collection of supporters, including royal dukes, dissenters, Paineite republicans, and humble subscribers. The cause was working-class education. It was given tremendous impetus by King George III, who, unlike conservative churchmen, was happy at the prospect of poor children being able to read. In 1805 he gave his patronage to the Quaker Joseph Lancaster, a pioneer of the 'monitorial system' of education, in which the pupils themselves, coached by a master, taught other pupils. The King's patronage and the consequent support given to Lancaster by his sons, the Prince Regent and the Dukes of Sussex and Kent, transformed the society into one of the

nation's most useful institutions. Before the government took an interest in education, it provided rudi-
mentary schooling for hundreds of thousands of poor
children.[15]

Radical support for a cause taken up by the monarchy may seem incongruous. Clearly, the aims and
motives of the royal family and the radicals who joined
the Royal Lancasterian Association (later the British
and Foreign School Society) were often at cross purposes. From the Crown's point of view, royal support
for Lancaster's experimental schools forged links with
advanced opinion, while promoting wider loyalty to
the throne. The radical tailor Francis Place, a member
of the Association's committee, had a different purpose. To him, the education of poor children was the
foundation of democratic reform, working-class dignity
and independence. Whatever the underlying politics of
the British and Foreign School Society, its supporters
were willing to set aside their differences because they
believed the cause to be of overriding social worth. The
educational charities of the early nineteenth century
provide telling proof that philanthropy was open to all
backgrounds and persuasions and could be justified on
grounds of democratic benefit and the promotion of
virtue.

The philosophy that inspired nineteenth-century
charity confirms that British society accepted social
hierarchy but put a premium on public spirit, the
removal of inequalities and the advance of disciplined
liberty, all essential republican principles. For many
Liberals, who carried forward the republican belief in
the importance of civic virtue, philanthropy was a
form of enlightened self-interest. John Stuart Mill
elaborated its political significance. 'The only security
against political slavery, is the check maintained over

governors, by the diffusion of intelligence, activity, and public spirit among the governed.' Without the habit of spontaneous voluntary action, he added, citizens 'have their faculties only half developed'.[16] With a deep-seated belief in the value of the individual and the social value of individual conscience, liberals and republicans, who were often at one in the nineteenth century, have always been more supportive of charity than socialists. Drawing heavily on radical traditions, they have never been obsessed by collectivism or class.

> 'Without the habit of spontaneous voluntary action, citizens have their faculties only half developed'

3

Working-Class Charity

Charity is largely driven by temperament. It is therefore suggestive to think of the history of charity not in terms of class, but more broadly as the history of kindness. This conveys the importance of philanthropy at all social levels and reveals its implications for individuals, families and communities. The standard definition of philanthropy or charity is love of one's fellow man, an inclination or action that promotes the well-being of others. It thus includes benevolence within classes as well as between them. Cast widely to include informal, domestic expressions of kindness, the philanthropic net catches virtually everyone at one time or another. Often the recipients themselves turned charitable in better days, for one of the striking things about kindness is its contagiousness. Many a workingman, for example, having had the hat passed round for his own emergency, gave generously to others in their time of trouble. The springs of charity are deeply rooted in such customs, often little more than impulses, and the needs and aspirations of people who respond to their difficulties and opportunities in a particular way, whether it be in the home, the pub or some grander social setting.

> *'Many a workingman... having had the hat passed round for his own emergency, gave generously to others in their time of trouble'*

The desire to protect one's community or to express one's aspirations through charitable work has always appealed across the social and ethnic spectrum. Charitable association has always been a most promising way for diverse minorities who are culturally vulnerable or politically isolated to forge a relationship with the wider society. Virtually all minorities in Victorian Britain had associations that addressed the needs of their distinct communities. Germans, Italians and French set up their own voluntary hospitals. Among Christians there were philanthropic emphases. Low church Anglicans favoured tract and Bible societies; Unitarians promoted educational causes; Congregationalists and Methodists were well represented in the temperance movement. Catholics founded innumerable charities that mirrored Anglican ones. Such institutions were necessary, if only as safeguards against proselytising evangelicals.

> '*Religious persecution, whether real or perceived, is a great incentive to philanthropic association*'

Religious persecution, whether real or perceived, is a great incentive to philanthropic association. Not surprisingly, Jews established some of the most distinctive institutions in Victorian Britain, from the self-consciously élite Board of Deputies to the humble *hevras*, which offered relief and community services to Jews who found themselves isolated in an alien culture.[1] Among today's most rapidly expanding British charities are those for the defence of Islamic and Muslim communities. In the five years between November 1996 and November 2001, the Charity Commissioners registered 385 Islamic and Muslim societies. (Over 100 Hindu and Sikh charities were also established in these years.)[2] The number of black

and Asian charitable workers today is living proof of
the fact that charity is not the preserve of the white
middle class.[3]

The availability of records of wealthy, middle-class
institutions has distorted our understanding of philanthropic experience. But the relative dearth of evidence
for working-class benevolence should not lead us to
underestimate its extent. In the past, as today, much
working-class charity was informal, spontaneous and
unrecorded, often merging with mutual aid.[4] Relatives
could be counted upon in time of trouble; running out
of them could be a shortcut to the workhouse. In
communities with a settled population, neighbours
also came to the rescue. Mrs Pember Reeves emphasised this point in her classic study of the London
district of Kennington before the First World War,
Round About a Pound a Week:

> should the man go into hospital or into the workhouse
> infirmary, extraordinary kindness to the wife and children
> will be shown by the most stand-off neighbours... These
> respectable but very poor people live over a morass of such
> intolerable poverty that they unite instinctively to save those
> known to them from falling into it.[5]

Apart from casual benevolence, which was wide-
spread, working men and women established soup
kitchens, washhouses, temperance societies, Salvation
Army shelters, boot and clothing clubs, ragged schools,
and funds for the victims of government repression.
Servants set up their own charities to look after
servants in distress. Navvies, who had a marked sense
of self-help, established sick clubs and visiting societies, complete with navvy officials. When the working
classes co-operated with wealthier neighbours, as in
hospital provision or foreign missions, their philanthropy often acted as a springboard into the existing
social system. This was particularly important in an

era when most working men and women remained outside the political nation. When the disenfranchised contributed to unemployment funds or passed the hat round for the relief of the Tolpuddle martyrs, their actions may be seen as an expression of radical politics by extra-political means.[6]

Middle-class women were also excluded from politics. For them, philanthropy was a form of self-expression, a readily available way of breaking out of the domestic routine and wielding influence. Charitable work was a lever which women used to prise open the doors closed to them in other spheres, for in its variety it was experience applicable to just about every profession in Britain. Charitable administration not only broadened the horizons of women but pointed out the limitations of their lives. Inevitably, it brought them into politics. Women trained in philanthropic societies, particularly those focusing on moral reform and education, were prominent among those who petitioned the House of Commons praying for the enfranchisement of their sex.[7] They often cited their contributions to charity as a justification of their right to vote. In turn, in their view, 'political power really does mean active benevolence'.[8] The movement for women's rights illustrates the affinity of charitable values and the political values of civil society. It is a telling example of how charitable organisation diffused the idea of participatory democracy by providing ideas and recruits to political campaigns.[9]

The assumption that charity is the preserve of rich conservatives has done untold damage. Clearly, active

> *'Charitable work was a lever which women used to prise open the doors closed to them in other spheres'*

benevolence justified the social standing and increased the authority of the propertied, but this is a partial view. Historians, perhaps unconsciously, have tended to perpetuate the view of many middle-class Victorians, who, according to the Victorian Chartist John Collins, had little idea 'that working men possessed any feeling or humanity'.[10] It was sometimes argued that the donations of the poor to charity were, as one writer put it, 'beyond all comparison the most important', for they were an expression of shared values and a common culture.[11] The press occasionally picked out humble philanthropists in the nineteenth century, to encourage others and show that no one class had a monopoly on good works. John Pounds (1766-1839), shoemaker and founder of ragged schools, and Sarah Martin, (1791-1843) seamstress and prison visitor, were perhaps the most celebrated. Their unsung successors can be found in myriad associations in poor neighbourhoods today, from playgroups to pensioners' clubs, where their work merges with daily life.[12]

The kindness of the poor to the poor was so extensive in the nineteenth century that Friedrich Engels declared that 'although the workers cannot really afford to give charity on the same scale as the middle class, they are nevertheless more charitable in every way'.[13] In the 1890s a survey of working-class and artisan families showed that half of them subscribed weekly to charity and about a quarter of them also made donations to church or chapel.[14] Well over half the income of several general hospitals came from humble contributors.[15] The League of Mercy, founded in 1899, raised £600,000 from artisan and working-class subscribers for the voluntary hospitals of London.[16] A London cleric put such practices in stark political terms at the beginning of the twentieth

century when he wrote that working-class philan-
thropy stood between 'civilization and revolution'.[17] Arguably, the philanthropy of the poor did as much as the philanthropy of the rich to subvert the revolutionary agenda that Engels and others so desired. Such a notion sheds a different light on the common assumption that philanthropy is subversive of working-class independence.

> '*working-class philanthropy stood between civilization and revolution*'

The degree to which charity saturated people's lives in the past, both givers and recipients, is difficult to imagine for anyone who has grown up in the shadow of the welfare state. A glimpse of the social microcosm of Rothschild Buildings in the East End, themselves a part of late Victorian 'philanthropy at four per cent', is telling. Apart from the extensive network of casual benevolence performed daily by the residents in this community, organised charities luxuriated. Run mostly by women, often with the assistance of the poor in the tenements, they included: Sick Room Helps' Society, Jews' Lying-in Charity, Israelite Widows' Society, Jewish Soup Kitchen, Whitechapel Children's Care Committee, Boot Club, Clothing Club, Children's Penny Dinner Society, Ragged Schools' Union, Bare Foot Mission, Children's Country Holiday Fund, Jewish Ladies' Clothing Association, and a Savings Bank. This concentration of 'charity, thrift, and paternalistic interference in the lives of the respectable working class', remarks the historian of the buildings, 'was to steal its way into every pore' of the residents, particularly the children.[18] This would not have happened, it should be said, if the 'respectable working class' had not co-operated or had not reaped some benefit from the charitable world that engulfed them.

The proliferation of charitable institutions in the nineteenth century reflected values that have come to be seen, misleadingly, as the preserve of the middle classes. Indeed, some historians define middle-class by reference to these values, having first defined the values as 'middle-class'.[19] But while the majority of charities which have left records behind were driven by the middle classes, the

> *'The privilege of giving is open to all'*

desire to protect one's community or to express one's aspirations through institutions appealed right across the social spectrum, from the aristocracy to the labouring poor. 'The privilege of giving is open to all' went a familiar Victorian saying.[20] The missionary and Bible societies were probably the most adept at bringing rich and poor into charitable communion. Working-class and artisan families contributed millions of pounds to these institutions in the nineteenth century.[21] However impoverished the Briton might be, the African or Asian could be made to look more wretched.

As a glance at working-class memoirs will attest, the poor knew the difference between 'deserving and undeserving' behaviour, and they did not need to be reminded that fitness, decency and self-help were wholesome. The leading historian of respectable society remarks: 'independence, self-reliance, and self respect, pursued through companionship, co-operation, and voluntary collectivism, were hallmarks of the Victorian working classes'.[22] Respectability was elastic, more an attitude of mind than a set of rules. Charitable institutions of all descriptions, whatever their size or social makeup, spoke its language. Whatever the background or social station of the giver, charity heightened status and self-esteem and offered a measure of respectability. It offered people in the most remote parts of the country opportunities to connect with their communities, to get outside themselves into wider experience.

Contributions to civic and charitable institutions had the great merit of encouraging men and women to feel part of the moral and social economy. One should keep in mind that Britain was administratively less uniform and centralised than continental countries, at least those conquered by Napoleon. In the mid-Victorian years, local authorities provided a multiplicity of goods and services that would astound many of today's local government officials, whose powers have been reduced so drastically by Parliament. Cities and towns in the four distinctive nations were jealous of their autonomy and proud of their local customs. Their leading voluntary institutions were pre-eminent symbols of civic virtue, often products of the new wealth created by manufacturing and industry. In the nineteenth century, a charitable hospital or a missionary society was the equivalent of an orchestra or football club today in the local support it attracted.

By the end of the nineteenth century, charitable enterprise was not only a sign of respectability and civic virtue but of national standing. Indeed, the Victorians equated their civilization with the high proportion of national activity given over to benevolent causes, just as a later generation would equate it with the welfare state. When Podsnap boasted to his foreign guest in *Our Mutual Friend* that 'there is not a country in the world, sir, where so noble a provision is made for the poor', he was trying to show his country to best advantage. When *The Times* announced in 1885 that London's charitable receipts exceeded the budgets of several European states, it was a source of national and imperial pride.[23] Ten years later the

Charity Commissioners gloried in their report 'that the latter half of the 19th century will stand second in respect of the greatness and variety of the Charities created within its duration, to no other half-century since the Reformation'.[24]

4

Voluntarism versus Collectivism

The very attainments of Victorian philanthropy made people more conscious of the social evils that remained, and less willing to tolerate them. Growing charitable receipts raised expectations of their successful application. But the persistence of poverty, particularly in its urban guise, was an acute embarrassment in a society of obvious wealth that prided itself on social improvement. The doubling of population over the reign of Queen Victoria and the intermittent periods of economic depression after the 1870s put additional pressure on voluntary services, exposing their patchiness and lack of co-ordination. With its marked local character, charity was most effective in a prosperous society characterised by vibrant and variegated provincial traditions. Towards the end of the century, it had not only to operate in a harsher economic climate but in a culture growing more homogeneous and national. The argument that charity was an expression of local or institutional democracy was less telling after the reform bill of 1884, which made the commitment to universal suffrage and representative democracy unstoppable.

The ideological battle taking place between voluntarists and the votaries of mass politics in the Edwardian years may be seen as part of the wider debate between the proponents of competing political visions of Britain that were often associated with classes or parties.[1] Those who sought a more radical and equitable distribution of wealth welcomed greater government intervention and set aside any worries about its effects on civic responsibility. At the other extreme were those advocates of charity who worried about a decline in moral activism, who thought an electorate clamouring for rights and entitlements from government would soon

> '*A social philosophy that neglected the duties of citizenship was one in which democracy would atrophy*'

deride the duties of citizenship. The fiercely individualistic Charity Organisation Society believed that government benefits would divorce poverty from morality and 'happiness' from 'duty'. A social philosophy that neglected the duties of citizenship was one in which democracy would atrophy. It was assumed that the more government took over from self-governing associations, the more individuals would have to turn to the state for benefits.

As a result of the growth of government responsibility in the social sphere, charity found itself on the defensive. Charles Booth's dispassionate survey *Life and Labour of the People of London* (1891-1903) and Seebohm Rowntree's *Poverty: A Study of Town Life* (1901), provided ammunition to those who were coming to the conclusion that benevolence was not scientific, nor comprehensive enough to address the causes of poverty. Fragmented by parochialism, traditional campaigners, many of them women, were at a disadvantage in an age of social science, mass politics and declining religious enthusiasm. (Did the decline in religion necessitate a greater role for government?) Voluntarists often assumed that distinctions between rich and poor were God-given and likely to persist. Conditioned by the Christian view that humanity was corrupt and poverty ineradicable, they found it difficult to compete with emerging secular philosophies that offered visions of mankind perfected.

Given the persistence of poverty in an era of unprecedented economic prosperity, the Christian analysis may seem less dated today. But in the early twentieth century, charitable activists looked increasingly old-fashioned to many social reformers in the Liberal and Labour parties. They laid themselves open to attack from intellectuals and socialists by their moral distinctions and their lack of social theory. That charities traditionally worked within the existing social structure made them anathema to many socialists, who assumed that in accepting social divisions philanthropists approved of them. To Marxists, with their dialectical eye on utopia, bourgeois philanthropists looked like the tired remnants of feudalism. Nor did they have much regard for the voluntary traditions of mutual aid within the Labour movement. Friendly societies and co-operatives lacked centralising power, and having been integrated into the mixed economy could do little, it was said, to challenge social injustice.

'The belief that poverty could be abolished presupposed an understanding of what caused it in the first place'

Against this background of opinion and the pioneering, albeit piecemeal, Liberal social legislation of 1905-11, charity found its status diminished. As the historian of philanthropy David Owen remarked:

When the focus shifted from 'the Poor' and what could be done to relieve their distress, to poverty and what could be done to abolish it, then it became inevitable that the State should intervene more decisively and that the scope of private charity should be correspondingly altered.[2]

The belief that poverty could be 'abolished' presupposed an understanding of what caused it in the first place. Here the voluntary sector, fragmented by its respective campaigns, was at a disadvantage. Pulling in different directions, charities were not well suited to an investigation of the relationship between poverty, old age and unemployment that had come into fashion in an era of improved social statistics. Nor did the claims of charitable campaigners to represent traditional institutional democracy have much meaning to ministers, who could argue that they represented the citizenry entire after the Representation of the People Act of 1918. The triumph of universal suffrage did not promote local democratic forms, rather the reverse.

Many of philanthropy's collectivist critics, by a sleight of mind, assumed that their more 'scientific' appreciation of the causes of poverty, made possible by social statistics, would lead to its elimination. All that was needed was the will of government and the right financial arrangements. The Fabian Sydney Webb, for one, took it for granted that collectivism, which he described as 'the mother of freedom', would ultimately triumph in social administration as in economic policy.[3] The state would streamline social life by a progressive takeover of those activities formerly provided by voluntary associations. In his idealised relationship between the individual and the state there was little need for the intermediary institutions of civil society, for the interest of the state and society were identical. In their writings, Webb and his collectivist allies helped to create the illusion that the state could transform society, as if by magic. They took it for granted that the poor themselves wished for an extension of statutory provision and that taxpayers would happily pay for it. The expectations thus aroused would place an enormous burden on later governments and form an ineradicable part of the prevailing climate of opinion in late twentieth-century Britain.

In the ever-greater politicisation of the health and social services that emerged in the early decades of the twentieth century, charity struck more and more commentators as not only inadequate but patronising. The Labour Party, which had grown out of a voluntary culture, became increasingly statist in outlook, a tendency that the two wars encouraged. Seen from socialism's dizzier heights, charity's personal approach to individual problems was backward, demeaning, and inappropriate to an urban economy. As Aneurin Bevan put it, voluntary traditions were little more than 'a patch-quilt of local paternalisms'.[4]

> '*Seen from socialism's dizzier heights, charity's personal approach to individual problems was backward, demeaning, and inappropriate to an urban economy*'

Charity's capacity to create personal bonds between volunteers and the needy struck some people as too closely identified with religious zeal. To others, not least 'masculine officialdom', the tendency to see social problems in moral and parochial terms was characteristically 'feminine' and therefore amateurish.[5] On the issue of philanthropy's place *vis-à-vis* the statutory authorities, the divide between the 'Beulah Land' of voluntarism and the 'Heavenly City' of socialism proved unbridgeable.[6]

The pioneers of state aid, from Edwin Chadwick to William Beveridge, did not much identify with those they sought to relieve. Beveridge distrusted 'the saving power of culture and of missions and of isolated good feelings'.[7] As Beatrice Webb once put it, '"a million sick" have always seemed actually more worthy of self-sacrificing devotion than the "child sick in a fever"'.[8] This impersonal approach to welfare, the belief in the efficacy of legislation, state intervention and large centralised bureaucracies was to become as compelling a remedy for social ills to its advocates in the twentieth century as individual service had been to the Victorians. The traditional liberal ideal of balancing rights and duties, as David Selbourne noted in *The Principle of Duty* was 'being gradually overwhelmed by a politics of dutiless right, a politics to which socialist aspiration made its own large contribution'.[9] The paradox was that twentieth-century collectivists had inherited from the Victorians a paternalist approach which exceeded that of the philanthropists they disavowed.

> *'twentieth-century collectivists had inherited from the Victorians a paternalist approach which exceeded that of the philanthropists they disavowed'*

5

The State Triumphant

The creation of the post-war welfare state signalled that in the longstanding battle between collectivism and voluntarism there appeared to be a clear winner. The ministerial, civil service state of Beveridge and the Webbs had routed the civic pluralism of Paine and Coleridge. To put it another way: indirect, representative democracy, expressed through Cabinet government, now reigned supreme in social policy over the spontaneous, pluralistic form of democracy that was immanent in the voluntary institutions of civil society. Local government fared little better than the charitable sector, for the loss of its principal service, the municipal hospitals, was a crippling blow to morale and recruitment. Nor did the Labour Party spare the mutual aid societies, which had given socialism its democratic infrastructure and moral centre.[1] Having subdued its rivals, central government was on its way to perfecting a form of executive democracy in which citizens were consumers of government rather than its producers.

> *'The war had boosted Labour's planning mentality, and... its leadership paid little heed to the... good offices of voluntary societies'*

The Labour government of 1945-50 was profoundly influenced by the extraordinary circumstances of the war, and it did not fully appreciate where collectivism would lead or how much it would cost, financially or culturally. The war had boosted Labour's planning mentality, and under the sway of historical materialism and collectivist ideals, its leadership paid little heed to the democratic impulses and good offices of voluntary societies with their ethic of personal service. Richard Crossman, Labour Secretary of State for Health and the Social Services in the 1960s, recalled the left-wing Labour view of interwar philanthropy as an 'odious expression of social oligarchy and churchy bourgeois attitudes. We detested voluntary hospitals maintained by flag days'.[2] Ironically, among the most outspoken critics of the proposals for the National Health Service were working people, who valued the democratic character and local control of *their* hospitals.[3] To the prophets of the New Jerusalem, who believed that social laws offered an ideological blueprint for the reconstruction of society, charitable campaigners were irrelevant, whatever their class.

There was, in fact, nothing inevitable about the shape of the nation's social provision, but the belief that history was moving in their direction had encouraged collectivists to disregard traditional practices in favour of root and branch reform. It was perhaps not surprising that they discouraged popular participation in their reforms, for if the triumph of their doctrine was inevitable, participatory democracy was pointless in any case. That deceptive civil service expression 'consultation' helped to paper over the cracks. Yet, as Crossman conceded: 'The impression was given that socialism was an affair for the Cabinet, acting through the existing Civil Service'.[4] Labour ministers simply assumed that the state was the embodiment of social good. They believed, in Crossman's words, that it was 'only through state action' that a transformation of society and a sense of community could be achieved.[5] Was the belief that citizens became moral agents through compulsory taxation to pay for universal benefits, which often accrued to those who did not need them, a deception? Few asked whether collective social properties existed. Socialists were so certain of it that they did not bother to provide the evidence.

Politicians and civil servants could justify greater state intervention in the social sphere simply on the grounds that the intermediate institutions of civil society had broken down during the war and were unlikely to recover. They could also argue that the Beveridge Plan was comprehensive and based on insurance principles, unlike charity which was patchy and selective. Yet, the growing identification of the central state with society not only discouraged pluralism and local democracy but politicised ever wider areas of social life. The Labour government introduced, arguably for the first time in British history, the sense that virtually everything was subject to politics. The belief that a programme of social progress would be set in train by the ministerial push of a button became a feature of British politics. The vast expansion of government services created a hybrid form of social imperialism, in this case turned inwards on little England. Indeed, the collapse of the Empire and the need to employ overseas civil servants at home helped the cause of administering what, to Whitehall mandarins, was a world of underlings.

> *'The vast expansion of government services created a hybrid form of social imperialism, in this case turned inwards on little England'*

For all the benefits—and they should not be under-estimated, particularly in health—collective social action left the individual disconnected, while the nationalisation of culture eroded former loyalties. Individuals were in some ways more impotent in an age of universal suffrage and parliamentary democracy than their disenfranchised ancestors had been under an oligarchic system.[6] How were they to create links between themselves and society in a political culture that placed so little value on individual effort and the intermediary institutions of civic life? Was the creation of such a bureaucratic welfare system an aberration in British history? Clearly, something fundamental was happening in a society, so voluntarist in the past, in which the burden of care shifted so radically to government, in which anonymous officials doled out the nation's capital in the name of 'the people', while individual service became characterised as a frill.

> *'Individuals were in some ways more impotent in an age of universal suffrage and parliamentary democracy than their disenfranchised ancestors had been under an oligarchic system'*

As if in compensation, politicians and social commentators sought to replace the sense of community, which people had built up in the past out of family life and local institutions, with a sense of national community, built out of party politics and central administrative structures. In passing social legislation, the government acted in the name of freedom, progress and social justice. But the more the government expanded its social role into areas that were formerly the responsibility of families and local associations, the more it diminished the duty, morality and nobility

of individuals. The more civil servants and politicians talked about 'the people' and the 'national community',
the weaker people and communities became. What had happened, for the best egalitarian motives, was a bloodless takeover of civic responsibility by faceless officialdom. The ostensible benefits made the takeover virtually irresistible.

> *'The more civil servants and politicians talked about the people and the national community, the weaker people and communities became'*

Gradually, the notion that a representative government had tutelary power over the citizenry took ever-greater hold, and with it the concept of ministerial responsibility for cradle to grave social provision. As Tocqueville had observed, a democratically elected government willingly works for the happiness of the citizenry, but 'it wants to be the only agent and final arbiter of that happiness'. It assures the needs and regulates the affairs of its citizens but turns them into dependent clients and fixes them 'irrevocably in childhood'.[7] In Tocqueville's analysis, this state of affairs would become most obvious in a régime that rose to power on the resentments of an oppressed class. As he saw it, self respect requires a high degree of self government in an egalitarian society. Without it, citizens unwittingly become their own oppressors. Arguably, his prophetic warning about the rise of a democratic form of benevolent despotism, built on class resentments and justified in the name of welfare, had come to pass, not in America but in Britain.[8]

Tocqueville's ghost hovered over the debate on the future of charity in the immediate post-war years. Voluntary institutions were in funereal mood. Some disappeared; many were nationalised, most notably over a thousand charitable hospitals; others shifted their priorities to avoid competition with government. Those with a traditional role in the social services, such as the Salvation Army and the city missions, soldiered on, there to catch the many people who fell through the state welfare net. Though little reported, the surviving institutions did not always disguise their hostility to officialdom, which the sometimes supercilious attitudes of politicians and civil servants excited. The King's Fund, which continued to represent the London hospitals, observed that the very word 'voluntary' was anathema to large sections of the National Health Service management.[9] Still, the democratic case for charity still surfaced from time to time. The ousted voluntary management of the Worcester Royal Infirmary lamented: 'We may not have the wealth of Government, nor the power to command a big staff, nor the funds to build all we require; but we have got a priceless asset, that as a people we want to maintain our democracy not only in a parliamentary way, but in our social service'.[10]

In the House of Lords in 1949, several peers, unsettled by the genie of big government that had been let out of the bottle, worried about 'the natural bias of the welfare state towards totalitarianism'. Voluntary action, as the Bishop of Sheffield argued, was one way of keeping it in check. The Labour peer, Lord Nathan, formerly a Liberal, joined in the paean of praise to philanthropy, describing charities as 'schools in the practice of democracy'.[11] Lord Beveridge himself, who the year before had published his book *Voluntary Action*, in which he called for 'fruitful co-operation' between the state and voluntary bodies, seemed to be having second thoughts about the impersonal bureaucracy that had come into existence. He was aware of the state's capacity to destroy 'the freedom and spirit ... of social conscience'.[12] Philanthropy would always be needed, he observed: 'Beveridge ... has never been

> 'Beveridge ... has never been enough for Beveridge'

enough for Beveridge'. Some things 'should in no circumstances be left to the state', he concluded, 'or we should be well on the way to totalitarian conditions'.[13]

The bureaucratic state, though impervious, proved less than monolithic, while the roots of civil society were so deep in the British soil that nothing short of totalitarianism could destroy them. By the standards of Soviet planning, British collectivism was a poor thing, *ad hoc* and full of gaps. Charity, though battered and diminished, survived. Apart from the older institutions that persisted, new ones emerged partly as a reaction to the very sense of powerlessness that individuals felt in the face of an imperfect democracy and the standardising tendencies of central government. The limitations of state social reform also held out the prospect of charities and government departments working together. Partnership precipitated changes within charitable bodies themselves, bringing many of them into line with modern conditions. Paradoxically, voluntary activity would be broadened, sharpened and enlivened by the very nationalisation of welfare that charitable campaigners had so often opposed.

The insensitivity of the state machine to individual need triggered a moral response from voluntary bodies, as well as relatives and neighbours. To a Treasury official, a hospital waiting list is an abstraction. To a charitable campaigner, it is an injustice. In *Voluntary Service and the State*, John Trevelyan argued that 'all possible steps should be taken by those who lead voluntary endeavour to build up an idealist philosophy for voluntary service of all kinds, a philosophy which will challenge the materialism so prevalent in our time'.[14] It was also thought that charitable service might serve as a challenge to the elevated notion of ministerial responsibility that had become so deeply ingrained. To the Secretary of the King's Fund, Arthur Ives, ministerial pretension had risen to the level of 'fiction'. 'We smile at the refinements of mediaeval scholasticism', he remarked 'but our own notions about the minister's ultimate responsibility are just about as far fetched'.[15]

Mutable, restless and fertile, the charitable sector discovered new needs and aspirations after the war. In the debate in the Lords in 1949, it was generally agreed that philanthropy would and must endure, for in a 'perpetually moving frontier' it was necessary, as Beveridge argued, 'to pioneer ahead of the state'. Partnership between volunteers and civil servants was seen as necessary to the democratic process. As Lord Pakenham put it:

> voluntary spirit is the life-blood of democracy ... the man who is proud to serve the community for nothing, is he whose personal sense of mission inspires and elevates the whole democratic process of official governmental effort'.[16]

One of the more pioneering roles of the 'junior partner' in the welfare world was to provide a critique of the state services. Increasingly, citizens would look to charities for mitigation of government policy.

6

The Democracy of
Charity Revived?

In the 1960s and 1970s, the welfare state came under criticism for red tape, secrecy, and an inability to provide sufficient participation for the public. Furthermore, as the historian of social policy Geoffrey Finlayson noted, the charge traditionally levelled against voluntarism was now levelled at the welfare state: that it could not cope with the volume of social need. 'The citizenship of entitlement had ... led to an overloaded state and a dependent citizen'.[1] Though the planning mentality was well entrenched, social engineering was increasingly out of fashion. By the 1980s, critics of statutory provision echoed arguments put forward by voluntarists a hundred years earlier: that the role of the state should be essentially enabling, to provide conditions in which alternative forms of welfare could flourish. The Whiggish assumption that British social provision was a linear progression to the welfare state was coming unstuck.

The strategic planning in state welfare provision which characterised the post-war decades ended in doubts, reassessment, and recrimination. Following Mrs Thatcher's victory in 1979, central government became an increasingly reluctant patron of the welfare state, and the emphasis in health and social services shifted to the pursuit of efficiency, private-sector

expansion and pluralism. Politics, it has been said, is
the organisation of hatreds. Just as the Labour Party
marshalled resentments against charity in the 1930s,
the new-model Conservative Party took its revenge on
the public sector in the 1980s (though Mrs Thatcher's
centralising tendencies won her few friends among
voluntarists).[2] As the costs and inefficiencies of government provision mounted, charitable enterprise
began to be taken far more seriously by politicians. At
the end of the 1980s, it was given an additional boost
by the collapse of the Soviet Empire and a new percep-
tion of civil society as a bastion of democratic values.

In the 1990s, leaders of the Labour Party, reeling
from Thatcherism at home and the collapse of socialism abroad, felt obliged to distance themselves from
their collectivist past. Notions of community and civil
society offered Labour a way of building a new constit-
uency. In 1998, Tony Blair pronounced that it was 'the
grievous twentieth century
error of the fundamentalist
left' to suppose that civil
society could be replaced by
the state.[3] In 1988, Gordon
Brown decried charity as 'a
sad and seedy competition
for public pity'.[4] In 2001, he
launched a campaign to
reinvigorate charitable service and civic spirit. As he
intoned: 'Politicians once thought the man in Whitehall knew best. Now we understand that the ... mother
from the playgroup ... might know better'. But Labour
shows little sign of withdrawing from its commitment
to state entitlements or lowering taxes in exchange for
charitable services. Charity, Brown insisted, was not
'a cut-price alternative to the state'.[5]

> 'Politicians once thought
> the man in Whitehall knew
> best. Now we understand
> that the mother from the
> playgroup might know
> better'

Labour thinking shows just how malleable a concept civil society can be. To many in the Labour movement, civil society is not a separate sphere, nor a check on arbitrary government. To the Blair government, as to previous governments, charities serve primarily as a way of implementing state social

> *'No recent government ... has had much regard for charitable independence'*

programmes more efficiently and cost effectively. Presumably, the use of voluntary agencies to do the government's bidding is the elusive 'Third Way'. In practice, it may be seen as a devolved form of socialism that turns the intermediary institutions of civil society into agencies of the state through contracts and financial control. Brown's initiative is arguably the latest illustration of the tendency of all post-war governments, sometimes consciously sometimes not, to undermine the independence of voluntary institutions. No recent government, it should be said, has had much regard for charitable independence, in part because voluntary institutions openly criticise government policy. Tocqueville's view that the state looks with ill-favour on institutions outside its control may be recalled. We might also recall his view that the citizenry are fearful of defending voluntary institutions, 'of which they stand in so much in need'.[6]

The generation that grew up during the heyday of the welfare state remains fearful of relying too much on voluntary provision and continues to look to government for essential services.[7] But the drift of opinion away from collectivism in the younger generation is potentially momentous, though not entirely reassuring to charitable campaigners. Many of them do not wish to take responsibility for erstwhile government provision; others do not wish to toe the line of government paymasters. Still, as a consequence of the cross-party embrace of charity, the public is becoming increasingly aware of the range and depth of voluntary activity. Charity can no longer be dismissed as merely an amenity or an impediment to social justice. The problems that afflict British society are now seen less in ideological terms than in the past, and they are thought to have solutions that require a greater degree of charitable contribution. For all its inventive intervention, the state is widely seen as too blunt and impersonal an instrument to provide security for British families without reinforcements from volunteers.

As the interest in civil society has proliferated in recent years, much of the tension between right and left over social policy has been defused. Yet a degree of tension between the state and voluntary sectors is inevitable. The essence of charity, like the essence of voluntarism generally, is its independence and autonomy—it is the antithesis of collective or statutory authority.[8] Government provision depends on compulsory taxation; it is not altruistic but materialist in conception. It is largely about furthering equality. Charitable provision, on the other hand, cannot be extorted by force; its proponents have usually been driven by individualist rather than egalitarian motives. Historically, the work of charity has been an expression of a liberal polity, at odds with an egalitarianism in which rights take precedence over duties. Distinctions between charity and government action are thus deeply rooted, not least in thinking about their respective roles and boundaries. The perennial

'where should the balance lie between the right to welfare and the virtue of charity?'

question remains: where should the balance lie between the 'right' to welfare and the 'virtue' of charity?[9]

The divisions between left and right that have bedevilled opinion about British charity will no doubt persist. But the continuing debate over social policy needs to be based on a better understanding of charity's underlying contribution to civic democracy. In a nation where there are more charitable volunteers than charitable beneficiaries, this contribution should not be underestimated.[10] The tendency to see philanthropy as a frill tacked on by the wealthy for selfish reasons not only overlooks the complexities of the subject but leaves the impression that kindness is beyond the capacity of rich and

> *'charity can turn privilege into virtue and propel people into good works who have little goodness in them'*

poor alike. Clearly, charity can turn privilege into virtue and propel people into good works who have little goodness in them. But who among us would wish to be administered by those who deny the sincerity of all public spirit or affection? Which is more subversive—and corrosive—to believe in altruism or to see it simply as a cloak of self interest? Even if altruism did not exist, it would be necessary to believe in it. Pessimists in power are prone to despotism.

To break down the tidy-minded half-truths about philanthropy, it is sensible to see it in its variety and contradictions, as an expression of a pluralistic society. As suggested, benevolence has as much to do with temperament as class; and the poor themselves have made a significant contribution to charitable traditions through their own efforts. In a society that prides itself on ethnic diversity, voluntary groups that provide a distinctive voice to minorities will become an increasingly attractive outlet for the expression of idealism and community spirit. Rethinking charity as a form of republican virtue may be a way forward. When seen as an expression of public spirit and participatory citizenship, charitable work raises fundamental principles about the relationship of the individual to the wider society. In a materialist society in which democratic values are thought to be in decline, a reappraisal of the epithet 'do gooder' is long overdue. Where charity is esteemed, citizens produce as well as consume government.

> *'The charitable impulse ... is subversive of the centralising state ... But over the years, government has done more to subvert philanthropy than the other way around'*

The charitable impulse has been described as subversive. Clearly, it is subversive of the centralising state and its penchant for social engineering. But over the years, government has done more to subvert philanthropy than the other way around. The attitude of charitable campaigners to the state in the nineteenth century has been likened to the revulsion felt by the curly haired boy in *Nicholas Nickleby*, as his mouth opened before Mrs Squeers's brimstone and treacle spoon. Today, in the scramble for scarce resources, charitable campaigners eat eagerly out of the government trough. In the mid-1980s, about ten per cent of overall philanthropic revenue came from government sources.[11] Ten years later, the figure stood at about 35 per cent.[12] The appetite for government funding has become so great that it is the question is now being asked whether charitable societies are in fact voluntary today?[13]

Since much of the erstwhile tension between left and right over social policy has been defused, a greater degree of partnership between the state and charities now seems inevitable. But partnership should not mean amalgamation. Achieving an equilibrium agreeable to all parties is a chimera. Tension between the two sectors, with their different agendas and contrasting democratic forms, is both desirable and invigorating. The expression of civic virtue, after all, requires more than sitting back, paying one's taxes and leaving the resolution of social problems to officialdom. A decline in voluntary activity is a measure of decay within a liberal society. In the end, the political maturity of a country is not measured by the size or form of government. It is measured by a polity that provides the conditions of liberty conducive to civil society and by what citizens willingly do for themselves and one another.

Notes

Foreword

1   Keynes, J.M., *The General Theory of Employment, Interest and Money*, London: Macmillan, 1936, p. 383.

1: A Great Army of Busybodies

1   Taylor, A.J.P., *English History, 1914-1945*, Oxford: Clarendon Press, 1965, p. 175.

2   See, for example, Stedman Jones, G., *Outcast London, A Study in the Relationship between Classes in Victorian Society*, Oxford: Clarendon Press, 1971; Donajgrodzki, A.P. (ed.), *Social Control in Nineteenth-century Britain*, London: Croom Helm, 1977; Rozin, M., *The Rich and the Poor: Jewish Philanthropy and Social Control in Nineteenth-Century London*, Brighton: Sussex Academic Press, 1999.

3   Castle, B., *The Castle Diaries 1974-76,* London: Weidenfield and Nicolson, 1980, p. 144, quoted in Harrison, B. and Webb, J., 'Volunteers and Voluntarism', in Halsey, A.H. and Webb, J. (eds.), *Twentieth-Century British Social Trends*, London: Macmillan Press, 2000, p. 614.

4   Grimond, J., 'Civil Society', *The World in 2002*, *The Economist*, December, 2001, p. 18.

5   See DeLue, S.M., *Political Thinking, Political Theory, and Civil Society*, Boston: Allyn and Bacon, 1997, p. 340.

6   Tester, K., *Civil Society*, London and New York: Routledge, 1992, pp. 5-6.

7   See Cohen, J. and Arato, A., *Civil Society and Political Theory*, Cambridge, Mass: MIT Press, 1992.

8   Harrison, B., 'Voluntary Action and Civil Society', p. 10, to be published.

9 Dahrendorf, R., *After 1989. Morals, Revolution and Civil Society*, London: Macmillan, 1997, p. 79.

10 *The Report of the Commission on the Future of the Voluntary Sector*, NCVO, 1996, p. 23.

2: Charity and Republican Virtue

1 Oldfield, A., *Citizenship and Community: Civic Republicanism and the Modern World*, London and New York: Routledge, 1990, p. 154, *passim*.

2 Prochaska, F., *The Republic of Britain, 1760-2000*, London: Penguin Books, 2000, pp. 91, 109.

3 Pettit, P., *Republicanism: A Theory of Freedom and Government*, Oxford: Clarendon Press, 1997, chapter 5. On American republicanism see Rodgers, D.T., 'Republicanism: the Career of a Concept', *Journal of American History*, 79, June 1992.

4 DeLue, S.M., *Political Thinking, Political Theory, and Civil Society*, Boston: Allyn and Bacon, 1997, pp. 340-03.

5 Skinner, Q., *Liberty before Liberalism*, Cambridge: Cambridge University Press, 1998, p. 17.

6 Dahrendorf, R., *After 1989. Morals, Revolution and Civil Society*, London: Macmillan, 1997, p. 78.

7 Keane, J., *Tom Paine: A Political Life*, London: Bloomsbury, 1996, pp. 116-17.

8 Paine, T., *Rights of Man, Common Sense, and other Political Writings*, Philp, M. (ed.), Oxford: Oxford University Press, 1995, p. 5.

9 Freedland, J., *Bring Home the Revolution: The Case for a British Republic*, London: Fourth Estate, 1998, p. 221.

10 Harrison, B., 'Voluntary Action and Civil Society', p. 9, to be published.

11 de Tocqueville, A., *Democracy in America*, [1835,1840] New York: Random House, 1981, p. 412.

12 See, for example, Hirst, P., *Associative Democracy: New Forms of Economic and Social Governance*, Cambridge: Polity Press, 1994; Gellner, E., *Conditions of Liberty: Civil Society and its Rivals*, London: Penguin Books, 1994. On the flexibility of Victorian charitable institutions see Morris, R.J., *Class, Sect and Party: The Making of the British Middle Class, Leeds, 1820 - 1850*, Manchester: Manchester University Press, 1990, pp. 161-68.

13 Owen, D., *English Philanthropy 1660-1960*, Cambridge, Mass: Harvard University Press, 1964, pp. 481-82.

14 See Prochaska, F.K., *Philanthropy and the Hospitals of London: The King's Fund 1897-1990*, Oxford: Clarendon Press, 1992, *passim*.

15 Prochaska, F., *Royal Bounty: The Making of a Welfare Monarchy*, New Haven and London: Yale University Press, 1995, pp. 34-35.

16 Mill, J.S., *Principles of Political Economy*, [1848] London: Penguin Books, 1970, pp. 312-13.

3: Working-Class Charity

1 Rozin, M., *The Rich and the Poor: Jewish Philanthropy and Social Control in Nineteenth-Century London*, Brighton: Sussex Academic Press, 1999, pp. 199-201.

2 I am grateful to the Charity Commissioners for this information.

3 On black volunteering see Hilton, R. and Davis Smith, J. (eds), *Volunteering & Society: Principles and Practice*, NCVO, 1992, chapter 7.

4 See Standish Meacham, *A Life Apart; The English Working Class 1890-1914*, London: Thames and Hudson, 1977, chapter 2.

5 Mrs Pember Reeves, *Round About a Pound a Week*, London: G. Bell and Sons, 1914 , pp. 39-40.

6 On working-class charity see Prochaska, F., *The Voluntary Impulse: Philanthropy in Modern Britain*, London: Faber and Faber, 1987, pp. 7-8, 27-31. See also, Prochaska, F., 'Philanthropy', in Thompson, M. (ed.), *The Cambridge Social History of Britain 1750-1950*, 3 Vols., Cambridge: Cambridge University Press, 1990, Vol. 3, pp. 362-66.

7 Blackburn, H., *Women's Suffrage: A Record of the Women's Suffrage Movement in the British Isles, with Biographical Sketches of Miss Becker* London: Williams and Norgate, 1902, chapter 4. See also Prochaska, F.K., *Women and Philanthropy in Nineteenth-Century England*, Oxford: Clarendon Press, 1980, pp. 227-30.

8 *The Westminster Review*, Vol. cxxxii, 1889, p. 279.

9 On this point, see Harrison, B., 'Voluntary Action and Civil Society', pp. 5-6, to be published.

10 Quoted in Harrison, B., 'Philanthropy and the Victorians', *Victorian Studies*, 9, 1966, p. 369.

11 *The Christian Mother's Magazine*, ii, October 1845, p. 640.

12 See Hatch, S., *Outside the State: Voluntary Organisations in Three English Towns*, London: Croom Helm, 1980, p. 51.

13 Engels, F., *The Condition of the Working Class in England*, Henderson, W.O. and Challoner, W.H.

(eds), Stanford: Stanford University Press, 1958, pp. 102, 140.

14 *Family Budgets: Being the Income and Expenses of Twenty-Eight British Households, 1891-1894*, 1896, p. 75.

15 Abel-Smith, B., *The Hospitals, 1800-1948*, London: Heinemann, 1964, pp. 250-51.

16 Prochaska, F., *Royal Bounty: The Making of a Welfare Monarchy*, New Haven and London: Yale University Press, 1995, p. 159.

17 Conybeare, W., *Charity of Poor to Poor*, London: S.P.C.K., 1908, p. 6.

18 White, J., *Rothschild Buildings: Life in an East End Tenement Block 1887-1920*, London: Routledge and Kegan Paul, 1980, p. 148.

19 See Wahrman, D., '"Middle-Class" Domesticity Goes Public: Gender, Class, and Politics from Queen Caroline to Queen Victoria', *Journal of British Studies*, 32, No. 4, 1993, pp. 396-432.

20 *The Juvenile Missionary Herald*, xvi, June 1878, p. 95,

21 The Methodist and Baptist missionary societies were among the most successful at eliciting contributions from the working classes, most of them from women and children. See Prochaska, F.K., *Women and Philanthropy in Nineteenth-Century England*, Oxford: Clarendon Press, 1980, pp. 82-85.

22 Thompson, F.M.L., *The Rise of Respectable Society*, London: Fontana Press, 1988, p. 353.

23 *The Times*, 9 January 1885.

24 *Forty-Second Report of the Charity Commissioners*, 1895, p. 17.

4: Voluntarism versus Collectivism

1   Harris, J., *Private Lives, Public Spirit: Britain 1870-1914*, London: Penguin Books, p. 16.

2   Owen, D., *English Philanthropy 1660-1960*, Cambridge, Mass: Harvard University Press, 1964, p. 525.

3   Webb, S., 'Social Movements', in Ward, A.W., Prothero, G.W. and Leathes, S. (eds), *The Cambridge Modern History*, 13 Vols., 1902-11, Cambridge: Cambridge University Press, Vol. 12, p. 765.

4   Bevan, A., *In Place of Fear*, London: Heinemann, 1952, p. 79.

5   Prochaska, F., *The Voluntary Impulse: Philanthropy in Modern Britain*, London: Faber and Faber, 1987, p. 74.

6   Owen, *English Philanthropy*, pp. 517-21.

7   Quoted in Briggs, A. and Macartney, A., *Toynbee Hall. The First Hundred Years*, London: Routledge and Kegan Paul, 1984, p. 61.

8   Quoted in Harrison, B., *Peaceable Kingdom: Stability and Change in Modern Britain*, Oxford: Clarendon Press, 1982, p. 259.

9   Selbourne, D., *The Principle of Duty*, London: Sinclair-Stevenson, 1994, p. 38.

5: The State Triumphant

1   See Green, D.G., *Reinventing Civil Society: The Rediscovery of Welfare without Politics*, London: IEA Health and Welfare Unit, 1993, chapter 10.

2   Crossman, R., 'The Role of the Volunteer in the Modern Social Service', in Halsey, A.H. (ed.), *Traditions of Social Policy*, Oxford: Basil Blackwell, 1976, p. 265.

3 Prochaska, F.K., *Philanthropy and the Hospitals of London: The King's Fund 1897-1990*, Oxford: Clarendon Press, 1992, p. 158.

4 Crossman, R., *Planning for Freedom*, London: H. Hamilton, 1965, p. 58.

5 Crossman, *Planning for Freedom*, p. 21.

6 Harris, J., 'Society and state in twentieth-century Britain', in Michael Thompson, M. (ed.), *The Cambridge Social History of Britain, 1750-1950*, 3 Vols., Cambridge: Cambridge University Press, 1990, Vol. 3, p. 63.

7 Quoted in Siedentop, L., *Tocqueville*, Oxford: Oxford University Press, 1994, p. 93.

8 Siedentop, *Tocqueville*, pp. 92-95.

9 See Prochaska, *Philanthropy and the Hospitals of London: The King's Fund, 1897-1990*, p. 166.

10 MacMenemey, W.H., *A History of the Worcester Royal Infirmary*, London: Press Alliances, 1947, p. viii.

11 *Parliamentary Debates*, 5th series, Lords, Vol. 163, p. 89, 105. On charitable societies as 'nursery schools of democracy' see Committee on Charitable Trusts, 1952-3, para. 53.

12 Beveridge, W., *Voluntary Action: A Report on Methods of Social Advance*, London: George Allen & Unwin, 1948, pp. 10, 318.

13 *Parliamentary Debates*, 5th series, Lords, Vol. 163, pp. 95-96.

14 [Trevelyan, J.], *Voluntary Service and the State: A Study of the Needs of the Hospital Service*, London, 1952, p. 17.

15 King's Fund Archives, Arthur Ives to John Trevelyan, 13 June 1950, file titled 'Social Service Enquiry (Trevelyan).

16 *Parliamentary Debates*, 5th series, Lords, Vol. 163, pp. 95-96.

6: The Democracy of Charity Revived?

1   Finlayson, G., 'A Moving Frontier: Voluntarism and the State in British Society Welfare 1911-1949', *Twentieth Century British History*, Vol. 1, No. 2, 1990, pp. 205-06; Finlayson, G., *Citizen, State, and Social Welfare in Britain 1830-1990*, Oxford: Clarendon Press, 1994, p. 366.

2   Prochaska, F.K., *Philanthropy and the Hospitals of London: The King's Fund 1897-1990*, Oxford: Clarendon Press, 1992, pp. 228-29.

3   Quoted in Harrison, B., 'Voluntary Action and Civil Society', p. 1, to be published.

4   *The Times*, 3 May 1988.

5   *The Times*, 11 January 2001.

6   de Tocqueville, A., *Democracy in America*, [1835, 1840] New York, 1981, p. 578.

7   See, for example, Taylor Gooby, P., *The Future of Giving: Evidence from the British Social Attitudes Survey*, Charities Aid foundation, 1993.

8   Gladstone,F.J., *Voluntary Action in a Changing World*, London: Bedford Square Press, 1979, pp. 3-4.

9   On this issue see Den Uyl, D.J., 'The Right to Welfare and the Virtue of Charity', *Social Philosophy & Policy*, Vol. 10, No. 1, 1993, pp. 192-224.

10 In 1980, it was estimated that around seven million people participated directly in the provision of charitable services, albeit most of them part time. See Gerard, D., *Charities in Britain: Conservatism or Change?*, London: Bedford Square Press, 1983, p. 18. For further statistics on volunteers see Harrison, B. and

Webb, J., 'Volunteers and Voluntarism', in
Halsey, A.H. and Webb, J. (eds.), *Twentieth-Century British Social Trends*, London:
Macmillan Press, 2000.

11 *The Times*, 17 December 1984.

12 *The Report of the Commission on the Future of
the Voluntary Sector. Summary of Evidence*,
NCVO, 1996, p. 18.

13 See Whelan, R., *Involuntary Action: How
Voluntary is the Voluntary Sector?*, London: IEA
Health and Welfare Unit, 1999.

CIVITAS: INSTITUTE FOR THE STUDY OF CIVIL SOCIETY

Trustees

The Lord Harris of High Cross (Chairman)
Professor Harold B. Rose (Treasurer)
Patrick F. Barbour
Professor Kenneth Minogue
The Hon. Justin Shaw
Sir Peter Walters

Advisory Council

Professor Norman Barry (Chairman)
Professor Brenda Almond (University of Hull)
Professor Peter Collison (University of Newcastle upon Tyne)
Professor Tim Congdon
Professor David Conway (Middlesex University)
Professor Antony Flew
Thomas Griffin
Dr R.M. Hartwell
Professor Barbara Ballis Lal (UCLA)
Professor Robert Pinker (London School of Economics)
Professor Duncan Reekie (University of Witwatersrand)
Professor Peter Saunders (University of Sussex)
Professor James Tooley (University of Newcastle upon Tyne)
Dr Jim Thornton (University of Leeds)

Staff

Director: Dr David G. Green
Deputy Director: Robert Whelan
Director of Community Studies: Norman Dennis
Director, Education Unit: Dr John Marks
Director, Criminal Justice Unit: Professor Malcolm Davies
Director, European Relations: Helen Brown
Senior Research Fellow: Patricia Morgan
Senior Fellow: Stephen Pollard
Editorial Assistant: Catherine Green
Project Manager, Health Unit: Ben Irvine
Project Manager, Family Studies Unit: Rebecca O'Neill
Administrator: Norman Wells

Independence: The Institute for the Study of Civil Society (CIVITAS) is a registered educational charity (No. 1085494) and a company limited by guarantee (No. 04023541). CIVITAS is financed from a variety of private sources to avoid over-reliance on any single or small group of donors.

All publications are independently refereed. All the Institute's publications seek to further its objective of promoting the advancement of learning. The views expressed are those of the authors, not of the Institute.